TRIPLE THREAT

Writers: Louise Simonson, Scott Gray,
Roger Langridge & Fred Van Lente
Pencilers: Rodney Buchemi, Craig Rousseau,
Jon Buran & Graham Nolan
Inkers: Rodney Buchemi, Craig Rousseau,
Jeremy Freeman & Victor Olazaba
Colorists: Guru eFX, Chris Sotomayor,
Sotocolor & Martegod Gracia
Letterer: Dave Sharpe
Cover Art: Karl Kesel & Pete Pantazis;
Clayton Henry & Guru eFX;
Tom Grummett & Guillem Mari; and Tommy Lee Edwards
Assistant Editor: Jordan D. White
Consulting Editor: Ralph Macchio
Editors: Nathan Cosby & Mark Paniccia

Collection Editor: Cory Levine
Assistant Editors: Alex Starbuck & John Denning
Editors, Special Projects: Jennifer Grünwald
& Mark D. Beazley
Senior Editor, Special Projects: Jeff Youngquist
Senior Vice President of Sales: David Gabriel

Editor in Chief: Joe Quesada
Publisher: Dan Buckley
Executive Producer: Alan Fine

Marvel Adventures Super Heroes #7

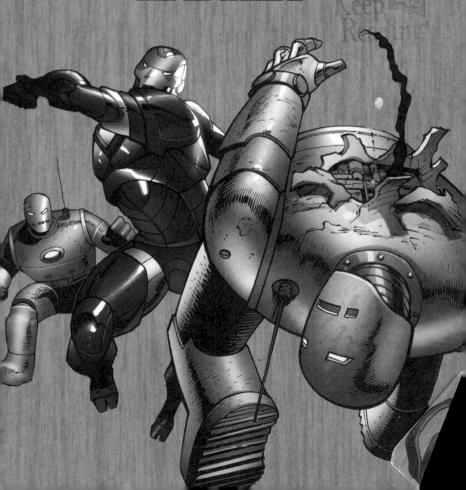

WHAKK!

THWOK!

WHOK!

Cease your *thievery*, craven varlets!

The safety of all who dwell on *Earth* is Thor's charge...

...and those who *threaten* that safety must answer to *me*!

DOCTOR DONALD BLAKE POSSESSES A MAGICAL CANE THAT TURNS HIM INTO THE ASGARDIAN GOD OF THUNDER...

THE MIGHTY THOR!

LIP SERVICE

LOUISE SIMONSON WRITER RODNEY BUCHEMI ART
GURU eFX COLOR DAVE SHARPE LETTERING ESPIN, KESEL & PANTAZIS COVER
TOM VAN CISE PRODUCTION JORDAN D. WHITE ASSISTANT EDITOR RALPH MACCHIO CONSULTING
NATHAN COSBY & MARK PANICCIA EDITORS JOE QUESADA EDITOR IN CHIEF DAN BUCKLEY PUBLISHER

THE NEXT DAY...

The *lions* are cool, Dr. Blake, but I can't wait to see the *Reptile and Amphibian House!*

Yeah? Why's *that?*

They have a *king cobra.* It's the world's most *poisonous* reptile. And a *gila monster.* And poison arrow *frogs!*

They have regular animals, too...but the *poisonous* ones are the *coolest!*

You had to *ask--*

Ooh!

What's *wrong?*

My...*lips!* For a second, it felt like a *bee* stung me.

SCHWIPPT!

SCHWIPPT!

SCHWIPPT!

The *Herpetarium* doors have opened!

There's been a *malfunction!* Everyone, please, walk toward the *exits!*

This happens just as we pass the enclosures of the world's most *venomous* creatures! *Not* a coincidence!

We have to *hurry!*

It's like a terrible *nightmare!*

Is it...? Jane, I--

--I need to get you **out** of here!

The doors are **locked!**

We're **trapped!**

Go **back** the way we came in! Head for the **entrance!**

Why's everybody **freaking out?** The snakes are probably **more scared** than they are!

But--aren't **scared** snakes likelier to **bite?**

Don? **DON!**

Jane! Don't **fight** the crowd. You could **fall!**

Go **on!** I'll **follow**--

Someone *opened* those cages...

...and since the controls are fully *automated*...

...the override command must have come from the *control room!*

BWOOM!

Don! D-Don!

This is where he *fell*... I *think!*

Omigosh, a *cobra!*

This is *awful!* And I don't see Don *anywhere!*

Is that... *Thor?* If the control room *door's* open, maybe Don's *inside.*

Patience, my darling. In a moment, the Cobra will **cease** to be a **menace!**

Keep back, Thunder god! W-where are you **taking** me?

There's a **storage room** in back--!

Storage room--?

With **equipment** for handling the reptiles, you silly woman! And food-- live **rats** and **bugs**--for the animals. More importantly, there's a staff **exit** into the park. And beyond that, escape... **freedom!**

You **heard** him, brother! Look! A convenient croc-net!

What are you **waiting** for? It's **showtime!**

I see the Cobra **agrees** with me.

Ohh. He's not badly **hurt**, is he?

Now you're worried about the **health** of that lame villain?

People are coming. You need to **kiss** my brother before it's too late.

Forget leaving his **transformation** to chance! **No snakes** or **frogs** in the room. Ah! A **rat!**

The perfect **form** for the mighty **Thor!**

He's **all right**, Jane.

He's just... **unconscious**, then?

Talk. Talk. Talk! Small wonder Odin still isn't a **grandfather!**

Kiss the girl, brother, and get it **over** with!

My hammer just **tapped** him. Gently.

HAHAHAHAHAHA!
ASGARD...
My favored son still moons over the mortal woman. Still, I find it rankles less... for now! She shows some spirit.
Never have I seen Loki so thoroughly snared by one of his own tricks!
And never have I been so greatly amused.
When it pleases me, I will release the trickster...in gratitude for the merriment he has just given me.
But I fear that in my mind that Loki will ever remain the Rat Royale of Ruses!
And once again, a great roar of laughter rings out across the battlements of Asgard.

Marvel Adventures Super Heroes #8

Captain...?

NO!

Holy cow, w-we actually *did* it--

He's *alive!*

Where am I? Who *are* you people? Where's *Bucky?!*

Captain, please try to stay *calm...*

I am *Major Sharon Carter* of the *Strategic Hazard Intervention Espionage Logistics Directorate.* We found you in the *Atlantic* a *month* ago. You're among *friends...*

Lock and *load*, boys, he looks *mad...*

The name's

CAPTAIN AMERICA!

Aargh!

Unngh!

"Strategic Hazard"...? Is that what you SS types are calling yourselves now?

If you're looking for a hazard, Fraulein, then this is your *lucky* day. Pleased to meet you...

Get off the road, flag-boy!

HONK! HONK! HONK! HONK! HONK! HONK!

It can't be...I must be dreaming...

Hey, move yer star-spangled tail, you whacko!

Whoa. There's a guy in need of some serious therapy...

Hey, that's a *buck-and-a-half*, pal!

A dollar-fifty... for a *newspaper*...?

And the *date*... the date is...

2009...?

Hey...dude... are you *okay*? You look majorly *freaked.*

I don't want to bum you out, but Independence Day is weeks away...

Wh-what...?

Bucky!

Ah, no... *Rick Jones.* Have guitar, will travel...

I'm available for kids' shows, bar mitzvahs and *costume parties,* which I'm guessing is where you're headed...

Sorry. For a second I thought...but no. I *remember* now. Bucky's *gone.*

Everyone I ever cared for... they must *all* be gone. I'm *alone...* ...strande the *futu*

"So they turned me into *something else*--a symbol for the *Allied Forces* to rally around...

"I became *Captain America.*

"I didn't fight *alone*, of course. I had the best partner a soldier could ever hope for--*James Buchanan Barnes.* The world knew him as *Bucky.*

"We tackled every monster the enemy could throw at us including the worst of them all--*The Red Skull.*

"We knew we had the Skull and all his ilk on the ropes-- the war was almost *done.* Soon we'd have a chance to *rest*...

"But that day never came.

"Did the Super-Soldier treatment *preserve* me somehow? Slow my *heart-beat?* Slow my *aging?*

"Maybe I'll never know for sure. But here I am."

The Neuro-Wave *paralyzes* any living thing in its path, Captain...

Nnnnghh!

ZREEEEEEE

I am *shielded* from its effects but you are not so *fortunate!*

As I *said*, I have no wish to harm you. In fact, this *vita-serum* will calm your raging body and save your *life...*

You'll be a very useful *tool* for *Hydra* once you've been *re-educated...*

You *know who we are*, don't you, Captain? Our... *name* has changed... our *uniforms* are new...

...but you *know who we are.*

Our *Supreme Leader* is looking forward to seeing you... Let's not keep him *waiting...*

FWANNNNG!

Eh?

Sorry to *interrupt*, dude-- thought I'd play your *bud* here a little *lullaby!*

Uhhh...

Much *obliged*, Rick.

You and I are going to talk some *more*, mister...

...*after you wake up!*

SHWOK!

AAAAAKK!

Maybe I should *thank* you. I wasn't sure what I could *offer* this new century...

But now I *know.* As long as there's scum like *you* still roaming the world--men who freely *destroy* and *terrorize* to achieve their aims...

Men who seek to *crush* the *ideals* that this country holds *dear*...

Then my war is *not over!*

Wa-hooo! Go, Cap!

Wow! I mean... *wow!*

You *tell* 'em, man!

Is that *really* Captain America?

Yeah... I think it *is*...

Ughh...

Cap! What's *wrong?!*

THE NEXT DAY...

So you've checked out okay, Cap?

Well, we "guys" do our best, Captain...

Major Carter! I want to apologize for my behavior yesterday--

You've got a lot of catching up to do, Captain. I've assigned a historian to bring you up to speed and act as your liaison. You can start today if you'd--

No thank you, Major.

Forget it. Like you said-- we needed the exercise...

Fit and fine, Rick. These S.H.I.E.L.D. guys know their onions...

I don't want to learn about my country from lectures-- I plan to discover it first-hand. I'll agree to a liaison, but I want it to be a man on the street...

What do you say, Rick?

Wha--?

It isn't just Captain America who needs to find his way in a new world...

C'mon, Rick... let's go see America.

I'm all for that, dude. What say we start at a steak house? I'm starving!

Steve Rogers has to do the same.

THE BEGINNING!

Oh, never mind! He can't have gone far!

Hmmm...

Hey, chum. Ever wanted to be in a cowboy picture?

Why, uh...er...

Swell. Put this on and stand on set over there, will you?

Good man.

Aha! There you are, you strange little fellow!

Karl Foeppl! At last!

Huh? Where'd he go?

What th--

CREEEAK

AAAAAHHHH!

I found another one! I'm pretty sure that's the last of them.

Swell.

So everything's fine now! You got your papers, Karl What's-his-name is in the clink. Don't I get a little "thank you"?

Oh! *I* got in *your* way, did I? Did it ever occur to you that you completely *ruined* my undercover exposé?

Of course, Miss Hepburn. Thank you for collecting the papers. Thank you for risking your neck.

Thank you for getting in my way. Thank you for letting the other spy escape...

How? By saving your life?

Listen, buster! We reporters represent *freedom of information!* Isn't *freedom* what this silly war is *all about?*

Reporters... you're all alike! You confuse *freedom* with the right to endanger *yourselves* and *others.*

If you *really* want to help the war effort, I'm sure there's plenty of *sewing* that needs doing...

Why, you... you're... you're...

⸝sigh⸝... gorgeous.

"Most great men and wo are not perfectly round their personalities, but instead people whose c driving enthusiasm is so g it makes their faults se insignificant."
--*Charles A. Ceram*

THE EN

Marvel Adventures Super Heroes #11

FIRE AND ICE

LOUISE SIMONSON WRITER JON BURAN PENCILER JEREMY FREEMAN - INKER
SOTOCOLOR COLORISTS DAVE SHARPE LETTERER GRUMMETT & MARI COVER
JOE SABINO PRODUCTION RALPH MACCHIO CONSULTING NATHAN COSBY EDITOR
JOE QUESADA EDITOR IN CHIEF DAN BUCKLEY PUBLISHER ALAN FINE EXECUTIVE PRODUCER

WHAM!

Blake is *safely hidden*, lad! Now we must insure *your* safety as well!

Son of *Odin!* I, *Bragmir*, challenge you to *single combat!* Turn to face me... and *perish!*

I felt the hand of my foster brother *Loki* behind that *blow*, young giant...

...and see his *sorcery* in the *axe* that you wield.

No *normal* weapon can *transform* what it touches into *brittlest ice!*

Young I am, and *small!* But I am no *runt* or puling *weakling* who needs *magic* to defeat you--

In time, Thor earned the magic hammer *Mjolnir.*

This is your *weapon*—to wield as Asgard's *god of thunder!*

But, like his father, Thor was *strong-willed.* Influenced by Loki's whisperings, Odin began to see this as *arrogance...*

I hereby banish you to *Earth!* There you will remain, in the guise of *Donald Blake,* a lame human *doctor,* to learn humility.

You will no longer have *Mjolnir...* nor will you retain any *memory* of your time as a *god.*

Odin changed Thor's *circumstances,* but not who he was *inside.*

Even as a *mortal,* Thor found ways to use his powers for *good.*

Despite Loki's effor to win Odin's *favor,* began to take pride Blake's accomplishme

And Loki's *hatred* and *ambition...*gre

The **fire demon** is done?

Nay...but his form on Midgard has been destroyed. He is driven back to **Muspelheim.** For the **moment,** Loki's threat is **ended.**

...ask your ...on, Odinson. I ...ht if I became ...oki, it would ...g me *honor.*

But Loki isn't what I *thought* he was. And I...have been a *fool!*

My foster brother is a clever *trickster* without honor... And though he has fooled **Odin** himself, he is *unworthy* of the regard of a *hero* of Jotunheim.

Hero? You mean **me**--?! But...I'm **no** hero.

My clan is **right** to despise me.

Then **they** are fools! Come, Bragmir!

What--? Is *that*--?

Marvel Adventures Iron Man #9

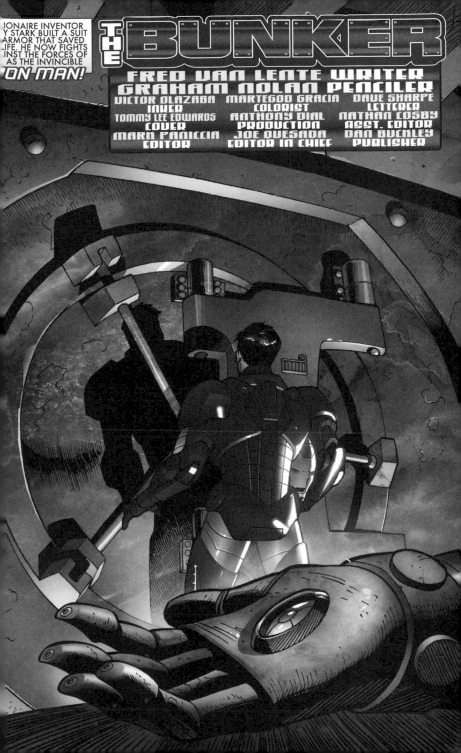

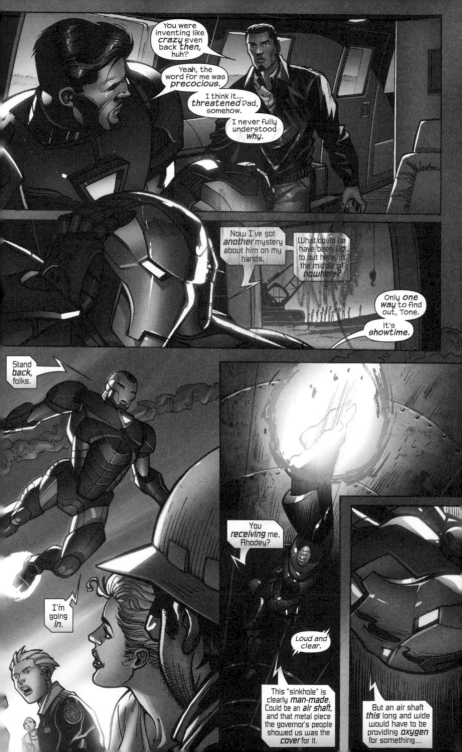

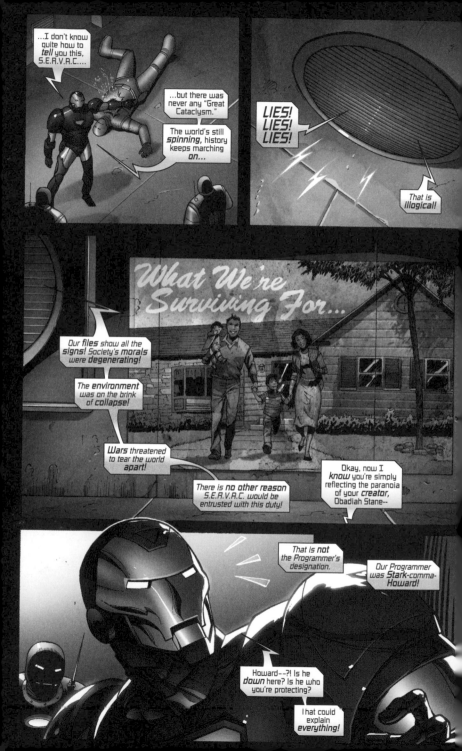

KLIK KLIK KLIK
KLIK

THUNK

HISSSSSSSS

RRAAAATTTLE

Hello.

My name is Howard Stark.

I have no idea who or even when anybody will be watching this.